UKULELE

Disney MARY POPPINS RETURNS
MUSIC FROM THE MOTION PICTURE SOUNDTRACK

Motion Picture Artwork TM & Copyright © 2018 Disney

ISBN 978-1-5400-4519-5

HAL•LEONARD®

Visit Hal Leonard Online at
www.halleonard.com

Contact us:
Hal Leonard
7777 West Bluemound Road
Milwaukee, WI 53213
Email: info@halleonard.com

In Europe, contact:
Hal Leonard Europe Limited
42 Wigmore Street
Marylebone, London, W1U 2RN
Email: info@halleonardeurope.com

In Australia, contact:
Hal Leonard Australia Pty. Ltd.
4 Lentara Court
Cheltenham, Victoria, 3192 Australia
Email: info@halleonard.com.au

(Underneath the)
Lovely London Sky

Music by Marc Shaiman
Lyrics by Scott Wittman and Marc Shaiman

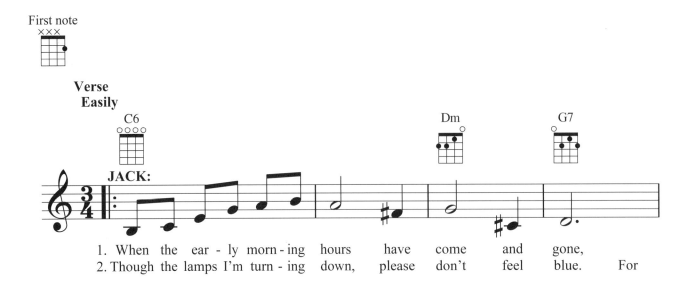

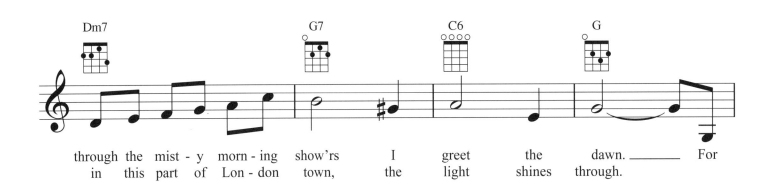

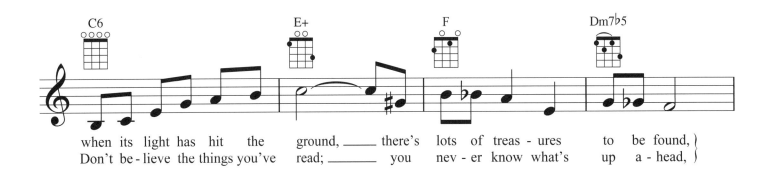

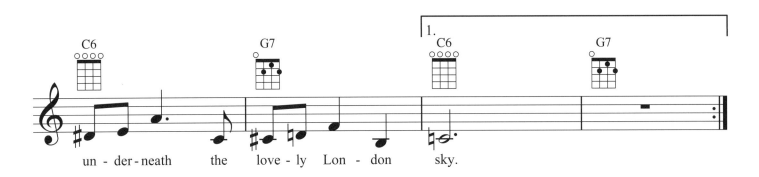

A Conversation

Music by Marc Shaiman
Lyrics by Scott Wittman and Marc Shaiman

First note

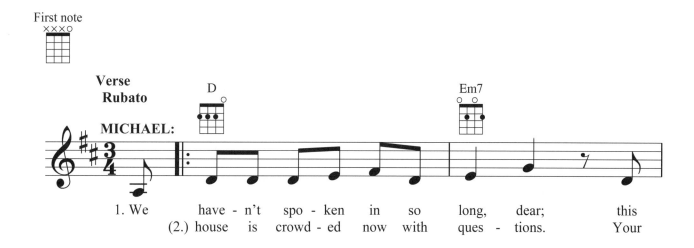

1. We have -n't spo - ken in so long, dear; this
(2.) house is crowd - ed now with ques - tions. Your

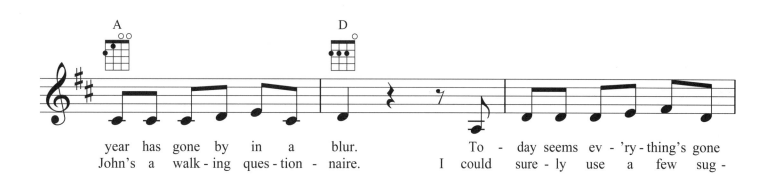

year has gone by in a blur. To - day seems ev - 'ry - thing's gone
John's a walk - ing ques - tion - naire. I could sure - ly use a few sug -

wrong here. I'm look - ing for the way things were. I
ges - tions on how to brush our daugh - ter's hair. When

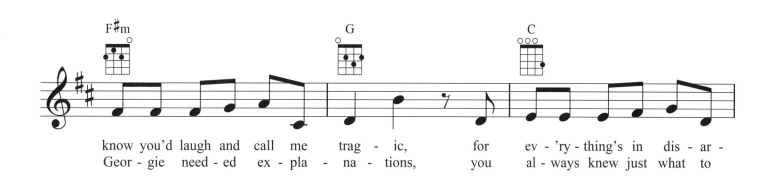

know you'd laugh and call me trag - ic, for ev - 'ry - thing's in dis - ar -
Geor - gie need - ed ex - pla - na - tions, you al - ways knew just what to

ray.   These rooms were al - ways full of mag - ic.   That's
say.   And I miss our fam - 'ly con - ver - sa - tions.   It's

1.

van - ished since you went a - way. _____

2.

2. This si - lent since you went a - way. _____

Bridge

Win - ter has gone, but not from this room.

Snow's left the lane, but the cher - ry trees for - got to bloom.

(Instrumental)   I'll

Outro-Verse

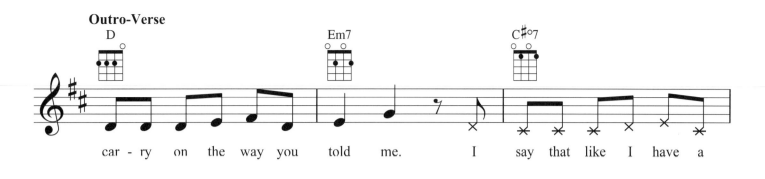

car - ry on the way you told me. I say that like I have a

choice. And though you are not here to hold me, in the

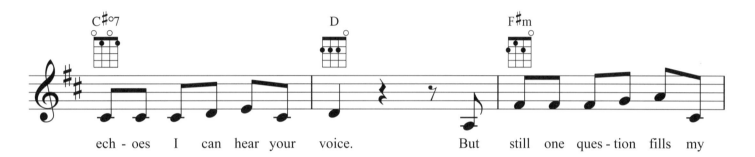

ech - oes I can hear your voice. But still one ques - tion fills my

day, dear, the an - swer I've most longed to know. Each

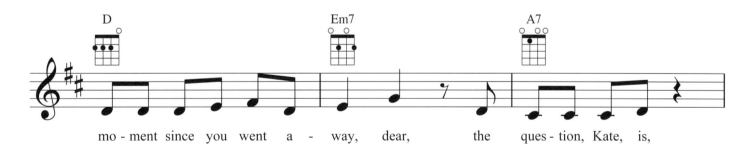

mo - ment since you went a - way, dear, the ques - tion, Kate, is,

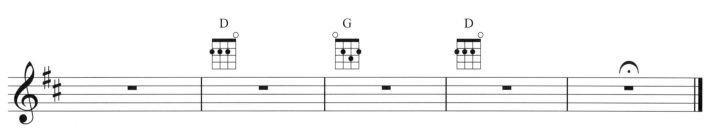

(Spoken:) "Where'd you go?"

7

Can You Imagine That?

Music by Marc Shaiman
Lyrics by Scott Wittman and Marc Shaiman

nev - er in - cor - rect, that you're far too old to give in to i - mag - i - na - tion...

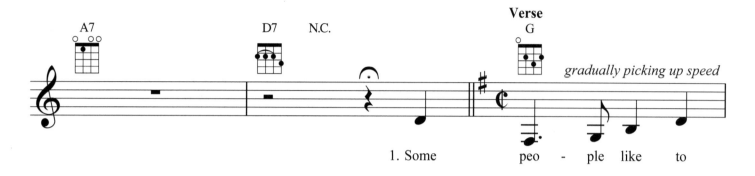

Verse

gradually picking up speed

1. Some peo - ple like to

splash and play. Can you i - mag - ine that? And

In tempo

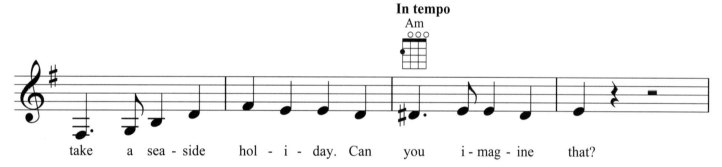

take a sea - side hol - i - day. Can you i - mag - ine that?

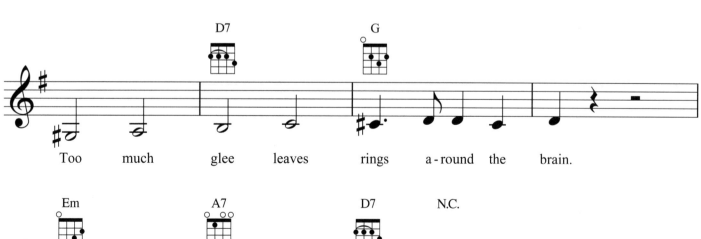

Too much glee leaves rings a - round the brain.

Take that joy and send it down the drain. Some

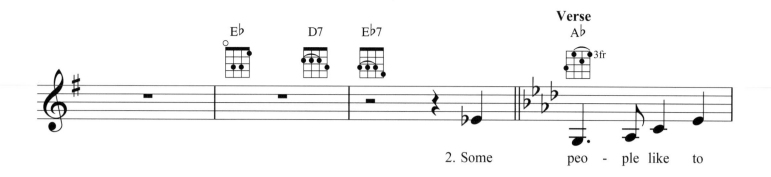

Verse

2. Some peo - ple like to

dive right in. Can you i - mag - ine that? And

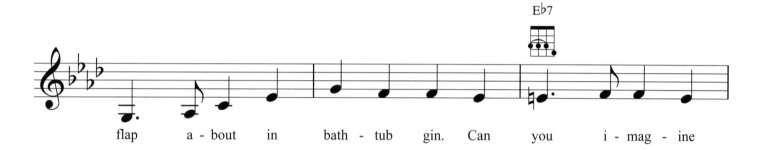

flap a - bout in bath - tub gin. Can you i - mag - ine

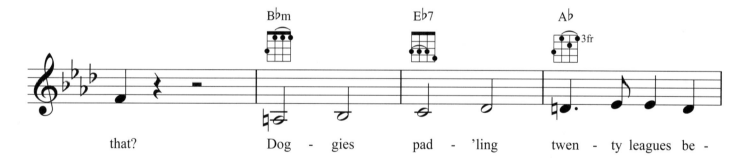

that? Dog - gies pad - 'ling twen - ty leagues be -

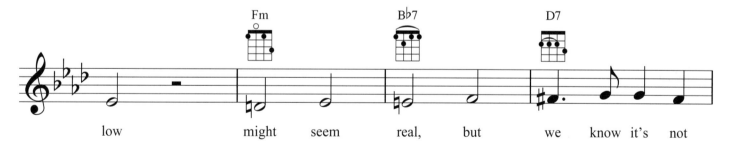

low might seem real, but we know it's not

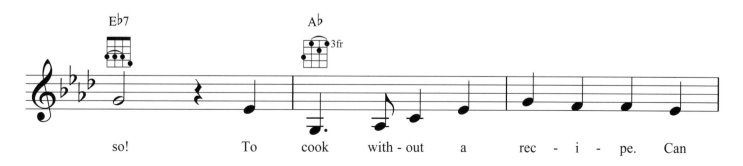

so! To cook with - out a rec - i - pe. Can

blue.   Yet some oth-ers wear an an-chor and they

sink in sec-onds flat!   So,   per-haps we've learnt when

day is done, some stuff and non-sense could be fun!

MARY & CHILDREN:

Can   you   i - mag - ine

Outro

that!

The Royal Doulton Music Hall

Music by Marc Shaiman
Lyrics by Scott Wittman and Marc Shaiman

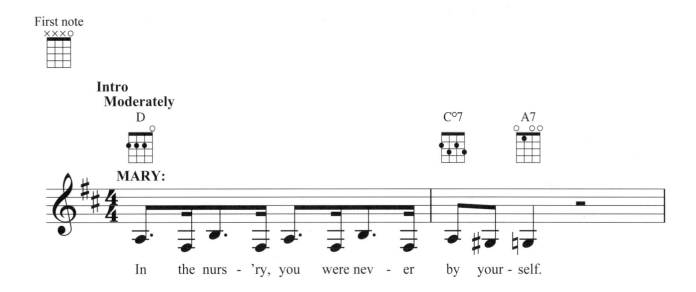

In the nurs - 'ry, you were nev - er by your - self.

There was quite an - oth - er world up - on your shelf,

where each day crowds make their way up - on the sun's de - scent to a

myth - i - cal, mys - ti - cal, nev - er quite lo - gis - ti - cal tent! 1. Yes, in this

Verse

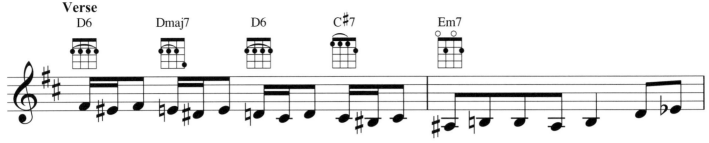

dear - ly dy - nam - i - cal, sim - ply ce - ram - i - cal Roy - al Doul - ton bowl, there's a

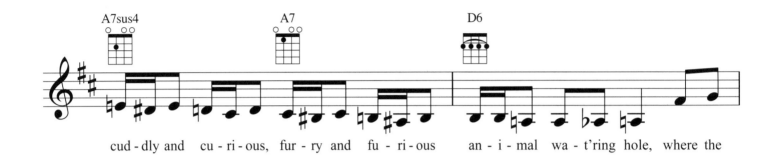

cud - dly and cu - ri - ous, fur - ry and fu - ri - ous an - i - mal wa - t'ring hole, where the

mon - keys and hum - ming - birds know the tunes and the words. Ev - 'ry beast large and small loves the

ver - y top drawer - a - ble, al - ways en - core - a - ble Roy - al Doul - ton Mu - sic

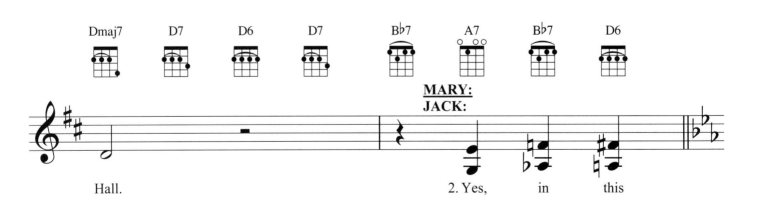

MARY:
JACK:

Hall.   2. Yes,   in   this

16

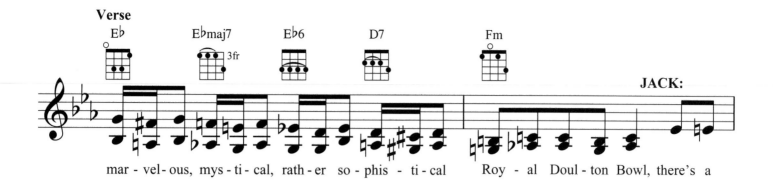

mar - vel - ous, mys - ti - cal, rath - er so - phis - ti - cal   Roy - al Doul - ton Bowl, there's a

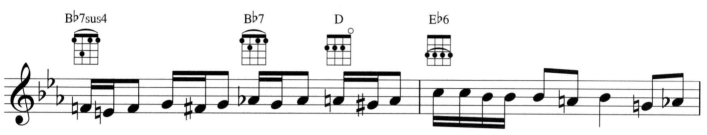

lot - ta birds queu - ing up, lot - ta hams chew - ing up   scen - er - y they swal - low whole. There are

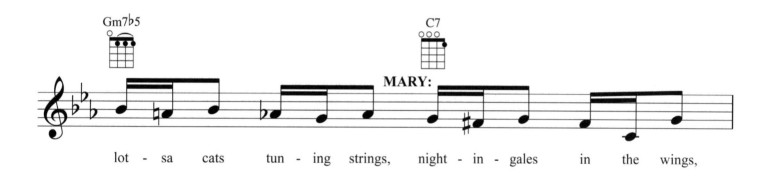

lot - sa cats tun - ing strings, night - in - gales in the wings,

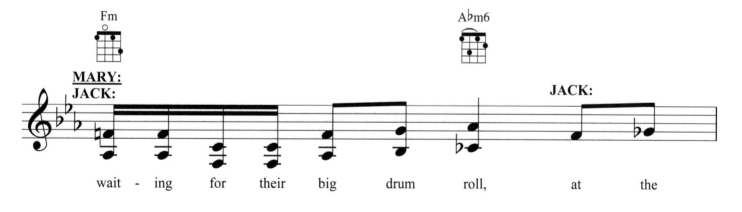

wait - ing for their big drum roll,   at the

sim - ply sen - sa - tion - al, stand - ing o - va - tion - al   Roy - al Doul - ton   Mu - sic

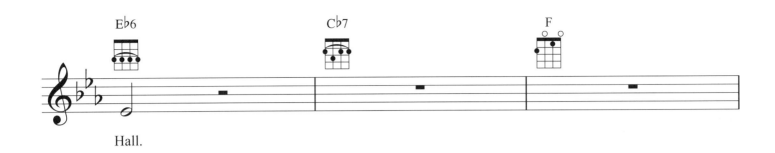

Hall.

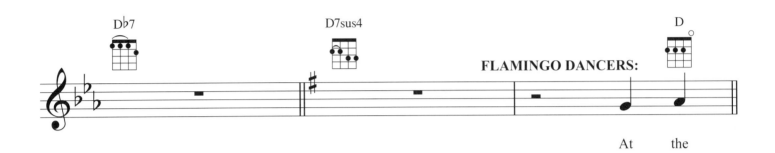

FLAMINGO DANCERS:

At   the

Outro
Faster

high - ly ac - claim - a - ble, near - ly un - tame - a - ble,

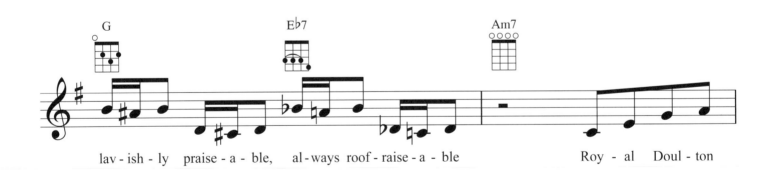

lav - ish - ly praise - a - ble, al - ways roof - raise - a - ble   Roy - al Doul - ton

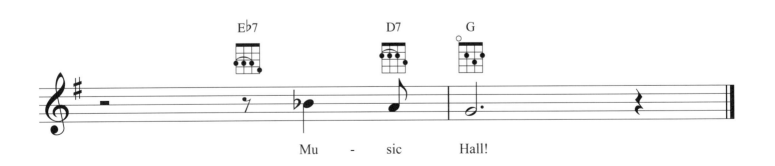

Mu - sic Hall!

A Cover Is Not the Book

Music by Marc Shaiman
Lyrics by Scott Wittman and Marc Shaiman

* Originally in D♭ major.

book, so o-pen it up and take a look, 'cause un-der the

cov-ers one dis-cov-ers that the king may be a

crook. Chap-ter ti-tles are like signs, and if you

read be-tween the lines, you'll find your first im-

pres-sion was mis-took, for a cov-er is nice, but a

AUDIENCE:

cov-er is not the book! Ta-ru-ra-lee ta-ra-ta-ta-ta! Ta-ru-ra-

up and take a look, 'cause un - der the cov - ers one dis - cov - ers that the

JACK: **MARY:**

king may be a crook. Chap - ter ti - tles are like signs, and if you

MARY:
JACK:

read be - tween the lines, you'll find your first im - pres - sion was mis -

took,   for a cov - er is nice, but a cov - er is not the

book!   **JACK:** *Shall we do the one about the "Wealthy Widow"?*

Verse

JACK:

MARY: *By all means!*   2. "La - dy Hy - a - cinth Ma-

caw" brought all her treas - ures to a reef, where she on - ly wore a

JACK: smi - le, plus two feath - ers and a leaf. So no one tried to

rob her, 'cause she bare - ly wore a stitch, for when you're in your birth - day

BOTH: **ALL:** suit, there ain't much there to show you're rich! Oh, a cov - er is not the

book, so o - pen it up and take a look, 'cause un - der the cov - ers one dis -

cov - ers that the king may be a crook. Ta - ru - ra - lee ta - ru - ra -

JACK: la. Ta-ru-ra-lee ta-ra-ta-ta! **ALL:** You'll find your first im-

pres-sion was mis-took, ya da da da, for a cov-er is nice, but a

cov-er is not the book! **MARY:** *Give us the one about the "Dirty Rascal," why don't you?*

JACK *(Aside, worried)*: *Isn't that one a bit long?* **MARY:** *Well, the quicker you're into it, the quicker*

you're out of it.

Verse

JACK: 3. Once up-on a time in a nurs-er-y rhyme, there was a cas-tle with a king hid-ing

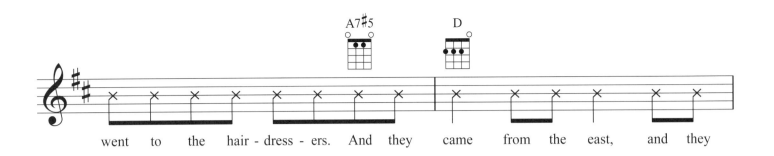

went to the hair-dress-ers. And they came from the east, and they

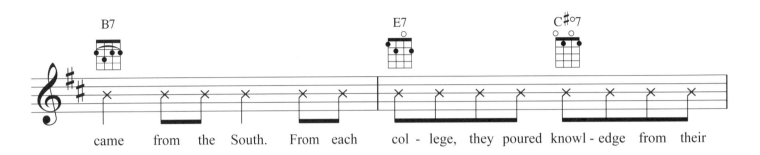

came from the South. From each col-lege, they poured knowl-edge from their

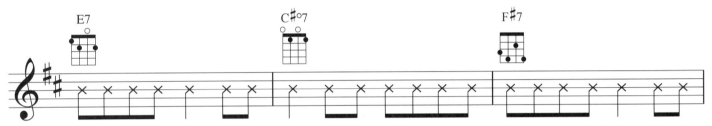

brains in-to his mouth. But the king could-n't learn, so each pro-fes-sor met their fate, for the

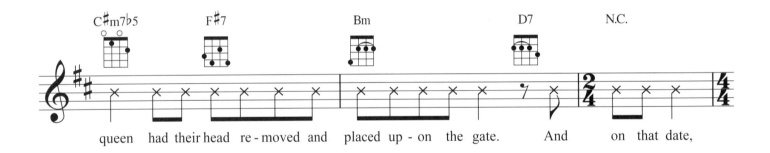

queen had their head re-moved and placed up-on the gate. And on that date,

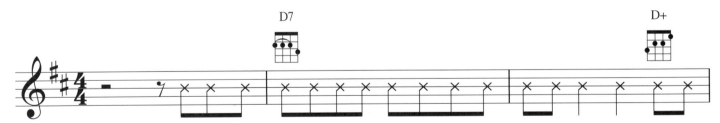

I state, their wives all got a note their mate was now the late great! But, then

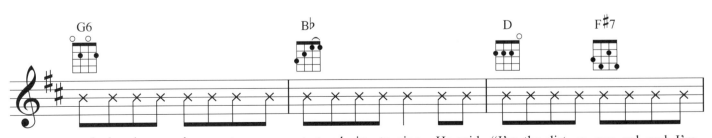

sud-den-ly one day, a stran-ger start-ed in to sing. He said, "I'm the dirt-y ras-cal, and I'm

here to teach the king!" And the queen clutched her jewels, for she

hat - ed roy - al fools, but this fool had some rules they real - ly

ought to teach in schools, like, "You'll be a hap - py king if you en -

joy the things you've got. You should nev - er try to be the kind of

per - son that you're not." So they sang and they laughed, for the

king had found a friend, and they ran on - to a rain - bow for the

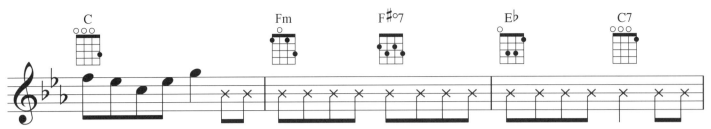

sto-ry's per-fect end. So the mor-al is, you must-n't let the out-side be the guide, for it's

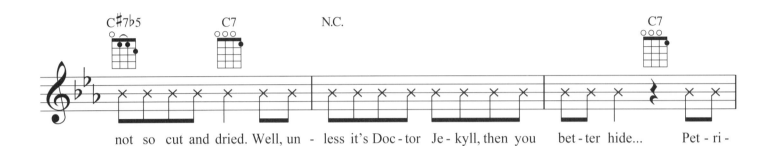

not so cut and dried. Well, un - less it's Doc-tor Je - kyll, then you bet-ter hide... Pet-ri-

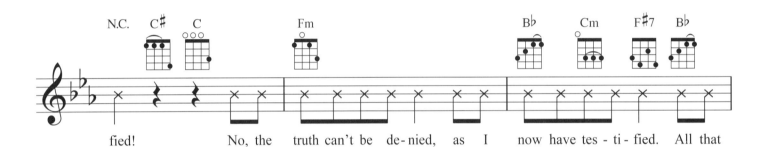

fied!   No, the truth can't be de-nied, as I now have tes-ti-fied. All that

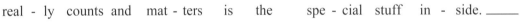
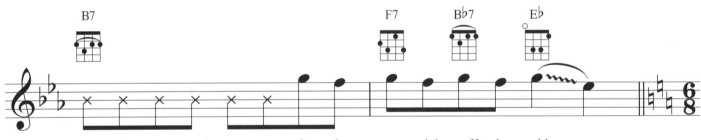

real - ly counts and mat-ters is the spe - cial stuff in - side. _____

Tempo I   **Outro-Chorus**

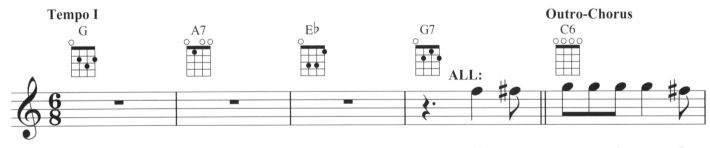

Oh,   a   cov - er   is   not   the

book, so o-pen it up and take a look, 'cause un-der the cov-ers one dis-

covers that the king may be a crook. So, please listen to what we've

said, and open a book tonight in bed. So one more time, before we get the hook! Sing it out strong: A cover is nice. Please

take our advice. A cover is nice. Or you'll pay the price! A cover is nice, but a

cover is not the book!!!

CHILDREN: Ta-ru-ra-lee ta-ru-ra-la. Ta-ru-ra-

lee ta-ru-ra-la. Ta-ru-ra-lee ta-ru-ra-la la la!

The Place Where Lost Things Go

Music by Marc Shaiman
Lyrics by Scott Wittman and Marc Shaiman

* *Originally in A major.*

Bridge

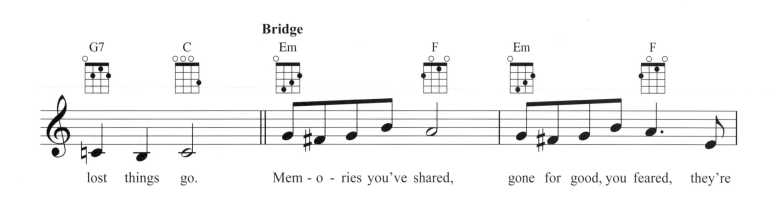

lost things go.   Mem - o - ries you've shared,   gone for good, you feared,   they're

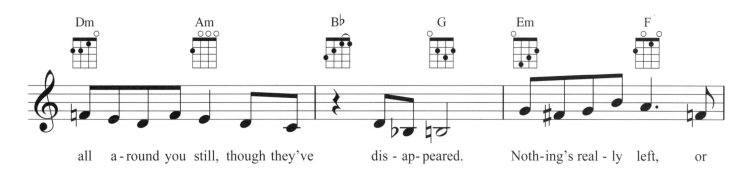

all   a - round you still, though they've   dis - ap - peared.   Noth - ing's real - ly   left,   or

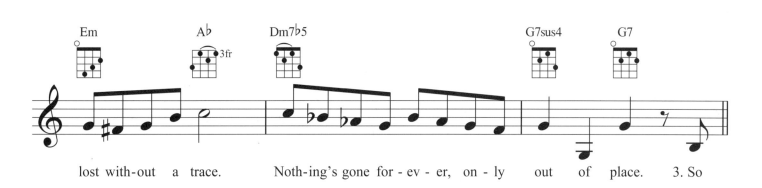

lost with - out   a   trace.   Noth - ing's gone for - ev - er, on - ly   out   of   place.   3. So

Verse

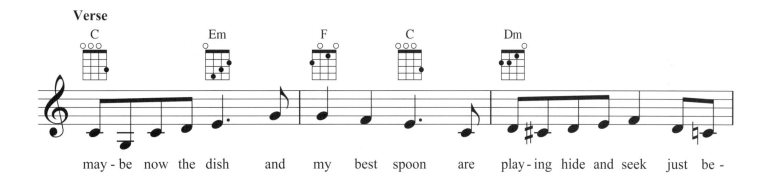

may - be now the dish   and   my   best   spoon   are   play - ing hide and seek   just be -

hind   the   moon,   wait - ing there un - til   it's   time   to   show.

Spring is like that now, far be-neath the snow, hid-ing in the place where the

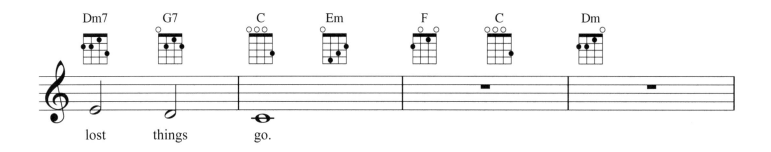

lost things go.

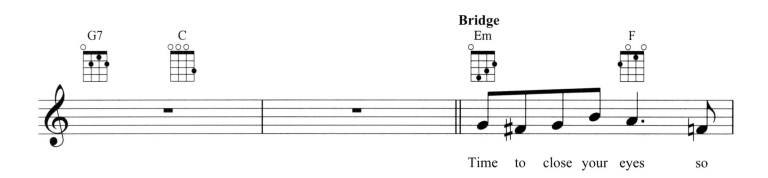

Bridge

Time to close your eyes so

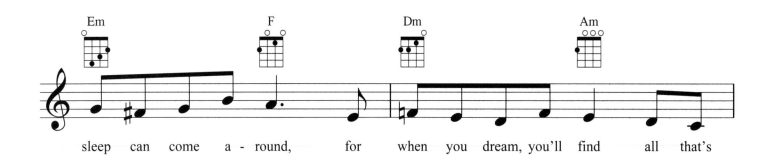

sleep can come a - round, for when you dream, you'll find all that's

lost is found. May - be on the moon, or may - be some-where new,

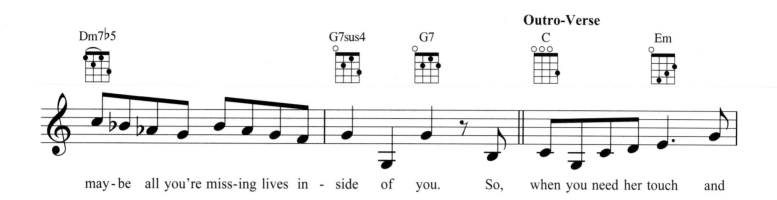

may - be all you're miss-ing lives in - side of you. So, when you need her touch and

lov - ing gaze, "gone, but not for - got - ten," is the per - fect phrase.

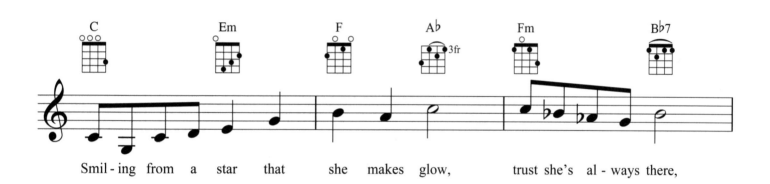

Smil - ing from a star that she makes glow, trust she's al - ways there,

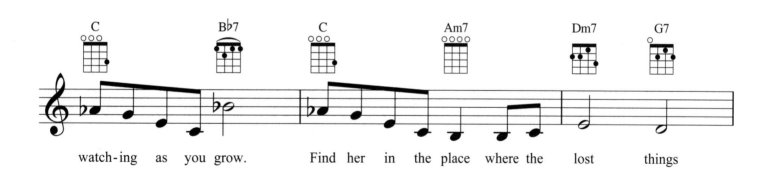

watch-ing as you grow. Find her in the place where the lost things

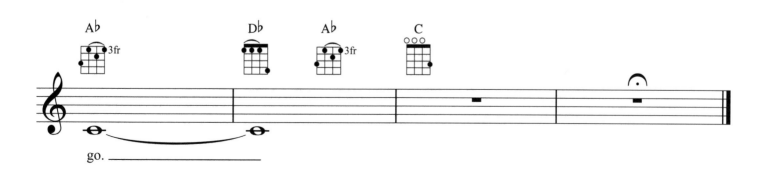

go. _____

Turning Turtle

Music by Marc Shaiman
Lyrics by Scott Wittman and Marc Shaiman

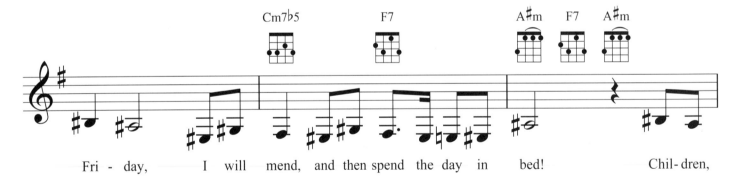

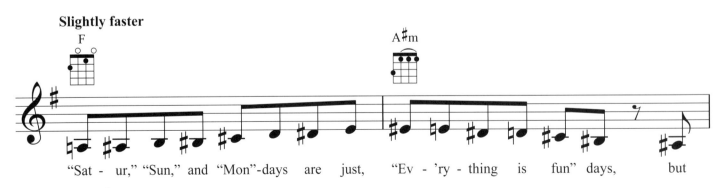

* Originally in E♭ minor.

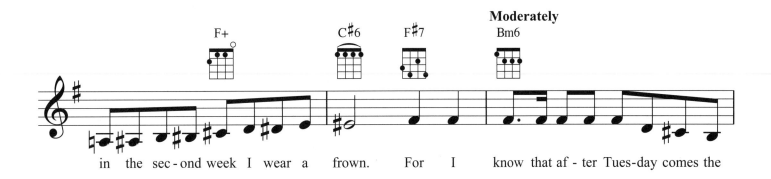

in the sec-ond week I wear a frown. For I know that af-ter Tues-day comes the

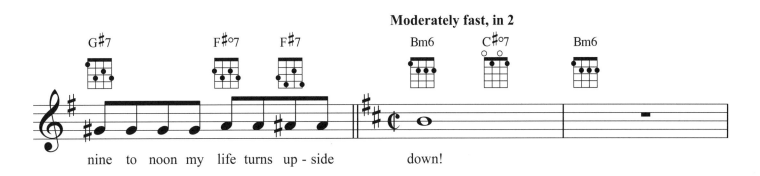

"Top - sy gets bad news" day. It's the dread-ed sec - ond Wednes-day! Where from

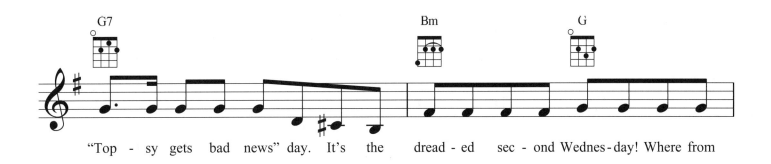

nine to noon my life turns up-side down!

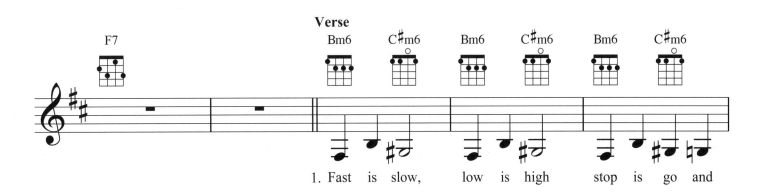

1. Fast is slow, low is high stop is go and

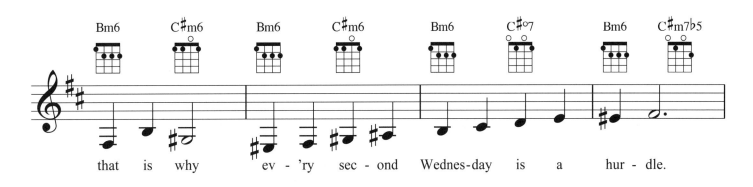

that is why ev - 'ry sec - ond Wednes-day is a hur - dle.

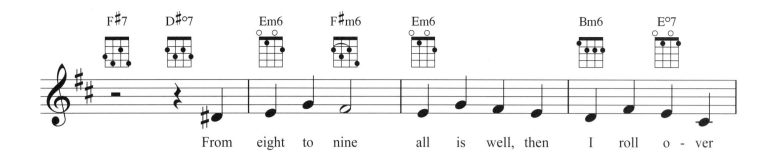

From eight to nine all is well, then I roll o - ver

on my shell, and all be - cause the world is turn - ing tur - tle!

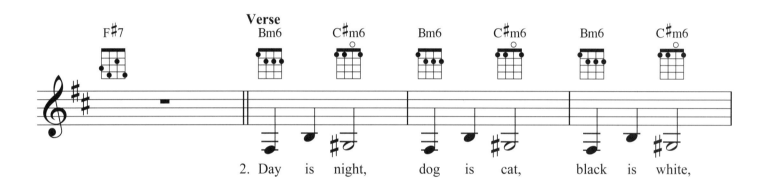

Verse

2. Day is night, dog is cat, black is white,

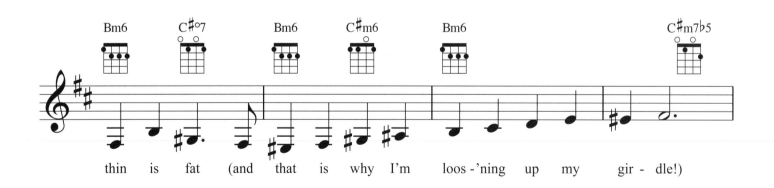

thin is fat (and that is why I'm loos -'ning up my gir - dle!)

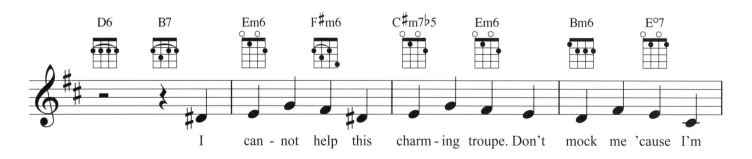

I can - not help this charm - ing troupe. Don't mock me 'cause I'm

in the soup. And why? Be - cause the world is turn - ing tur - tle!

Bridge

Oh, woe is me, I'm as op - po-site as I can be! I

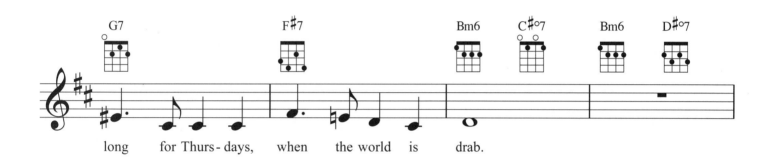

long for Thurs - days, when the world is drab.

When will it cease? Now my life re - sem - bles "War and Peace." (That

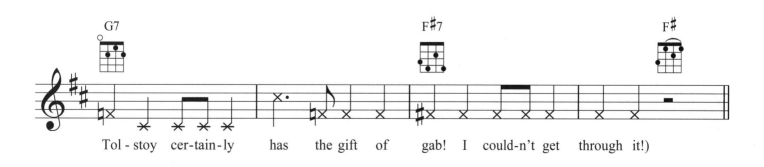

Tol - stoy cer-tain-ly has the gift of gab! I could-n't get through it!)

Verse

3. Bot - tom's top,   yin is yang,   peace and qui - et's *sturm und drang.*

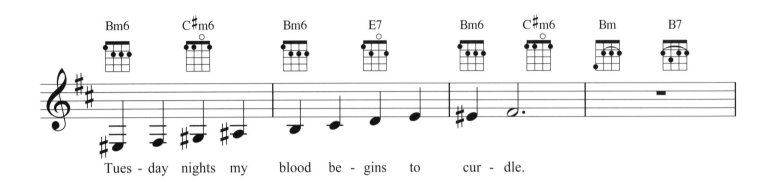

Tues - day nights my   blood be - gins to   cur - dle.

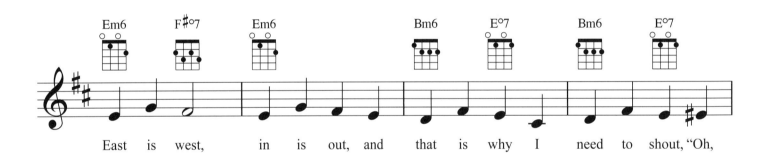

East is west,   in is out, and   that is why I   need to shout, "Oh,

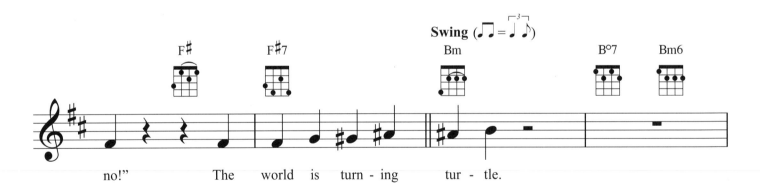

no!"   The world is turn - ing   tur - tle.

Bridge

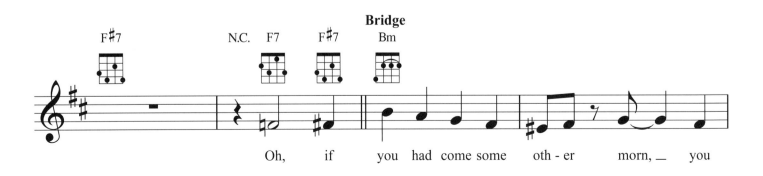

Oh,   if you had come some   oth - er   morn, __ you

would-n't have found me so for - lorn, __ but since the day that

I was born __ sec - ond Wednes-days are on the fritz. __ I

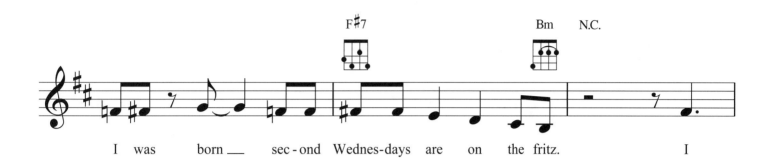

could-n't mend this to save my soul. __ If this keeps up, I'll

dig a hole. __ You say life's a cher - ry bowl, __ but

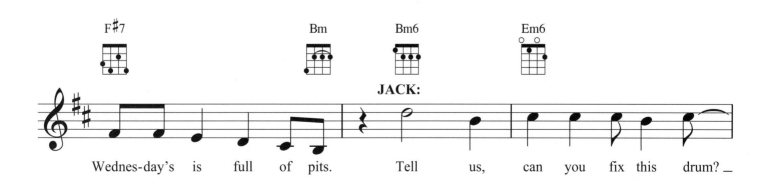

JACK:

Wednes-day's is full of pits. Tell us, can you fix this drum? __

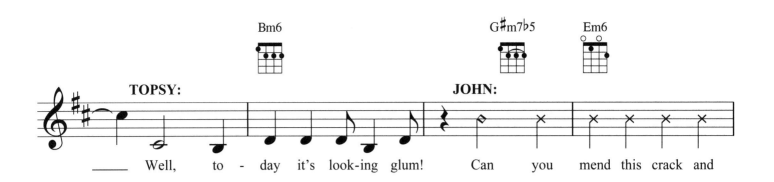

TOPSY: JOHN:

_____ Well, to - day it's look-ing glum! Can you mend this crack and

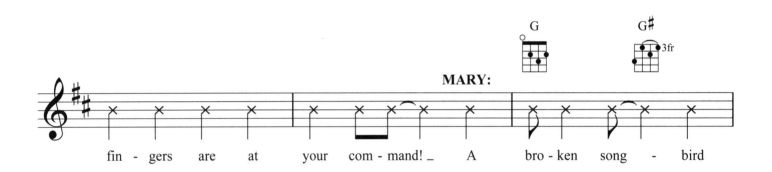

ANNABEL: TOPSY: JACK & CHILDREN:

bro - ken string? _ Well, per - haps if you all lend a hand. _ Our

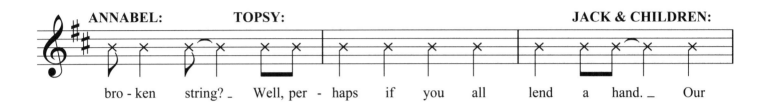

MARY:

fin - gers are at your com - mand! _ A bro - ken song - bird

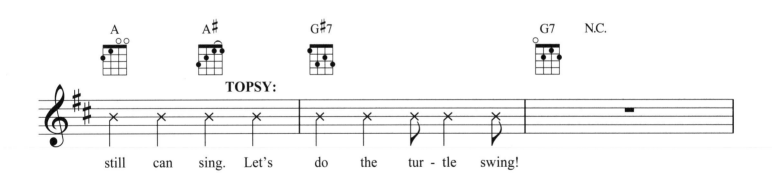

TOPSY:

still can sing. Let's do the tur - tle swing!

Straight 8ths

(Instrumental)

Bridge

Oh, woe is me. Now I'm on my head. How can it be? Well,

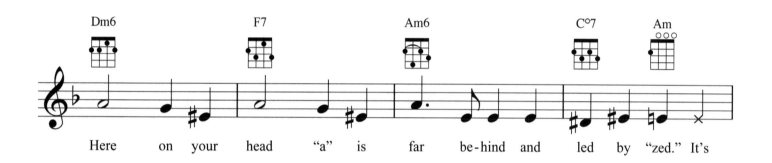

you say "woe" but I say "luck - y you!" Luck - y me? Yes!

Here on your head "a" is far be-hind and led by "zed." It's

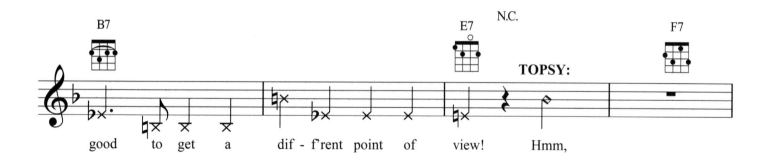

good to get a dif - f'rent point of view! Hmm,

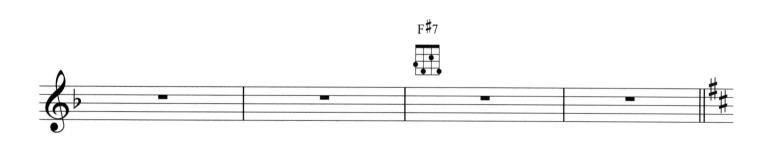

Outro

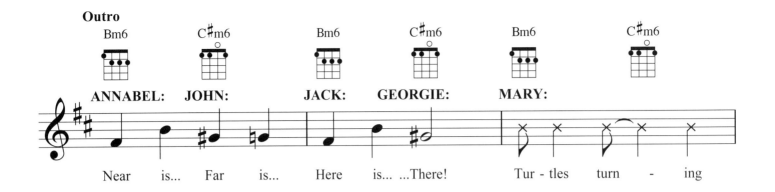

Near is... Far is... Here is... ...There! Tur - tles turn - ing

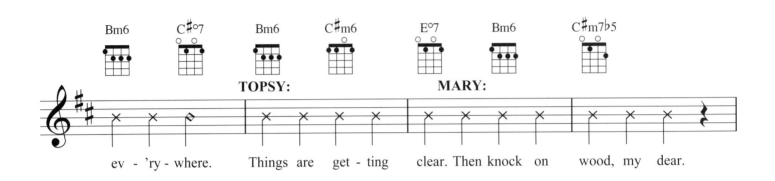

ev - 'ry - where. Things are get - ting clear. Then knock on wood, my dear.

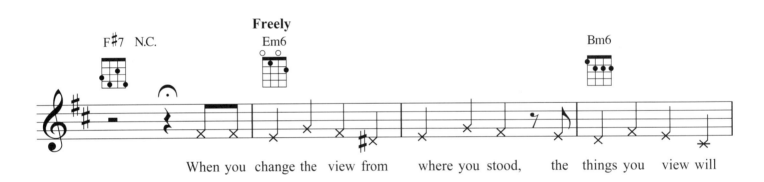

Freely

When you change the view from where you stood, the things you view will

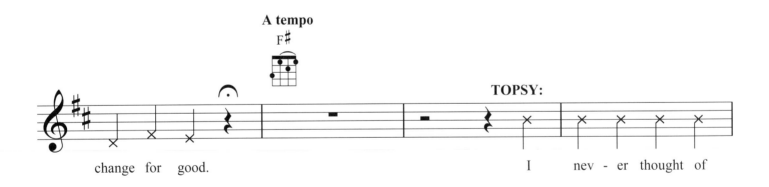

A tempo

change for good. I nev - er thought of

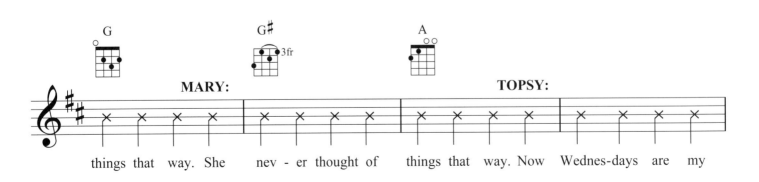

things that way. She nev - er thought of things that way. Now Wednes-days are my

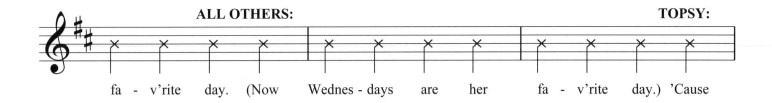

fa - v'rite day. (Now   Wednes - days   are   her   fa - v'rite day.) 'Cause

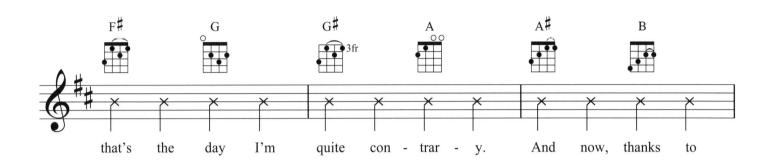

that's   the   day   I'm   quite con - trar - y.   And   now, thanks   to

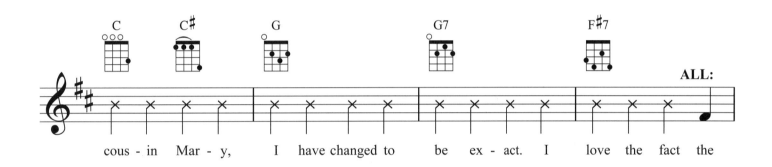

cous - in   Mar - y,   I   have changed to   be ex - act.   I   love the fact the

Slightly faster ($\sqcap = \overset{3}{\sqcap}$)

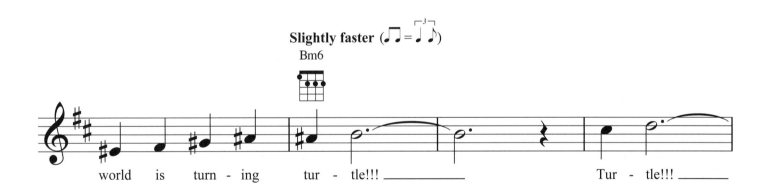

world   is   turn - ing   tur - tle!!! _____   Tur - tle!!! _____

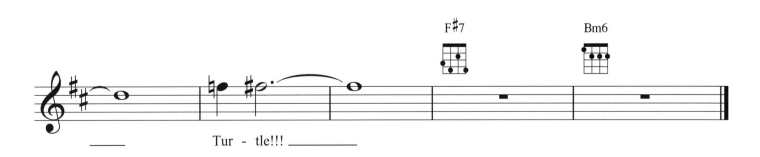

_____   Tur - tle!!! _____

Trip a Little Light Fantastic

Music by Marc Shaiman
Lyrics by Scott Wittman and Marc Shaiman

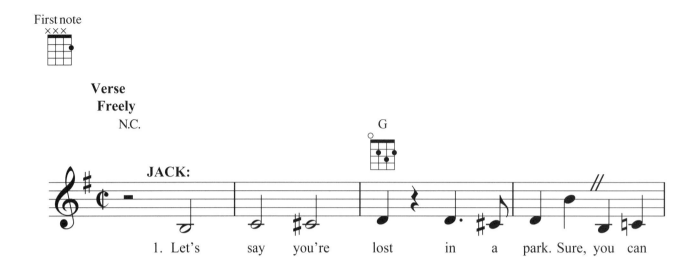

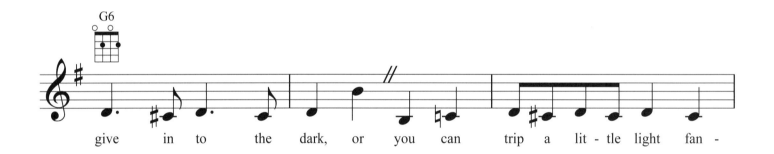

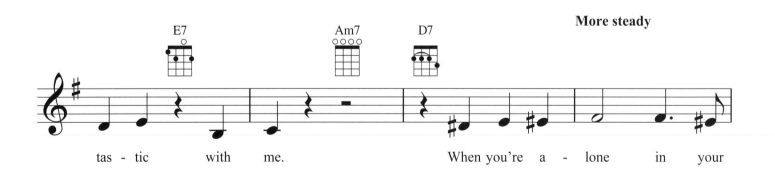

trip a lit - tle light fan - tas - tic with me.

Bridge
Gradually faster

For if you hide un - der the cov - ers you might

nev - er see the day. But if a spark can start in -

side your heart, then you can al - ways find the way. So when

Chorus
Moderately, in 2

life is get - tin' drear - y, just pre - tend that you're a

leer - ie as you trip a lit - tle light fan - tas - tic with

Slightly faster

G   Am7   Dmaj7   Eb7

JACK:

me.   2. Now when you're

Verse

Ab

stuck   in   the mist, sure, you can   strug - gle and re -

F7

sist,   or   you   can trip a lit - tle light fan - tas - tic   with

Bbm7   Eb7

me.   Now, say you're lost   in the crowd, well, you can

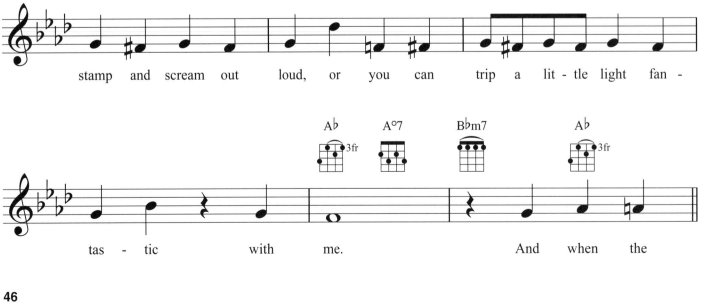

stamp and scream out loud, or you can trip a lit - tle light fan -

Ab   A°7   Bbm7   Ab

tas - tic with me.   And when the

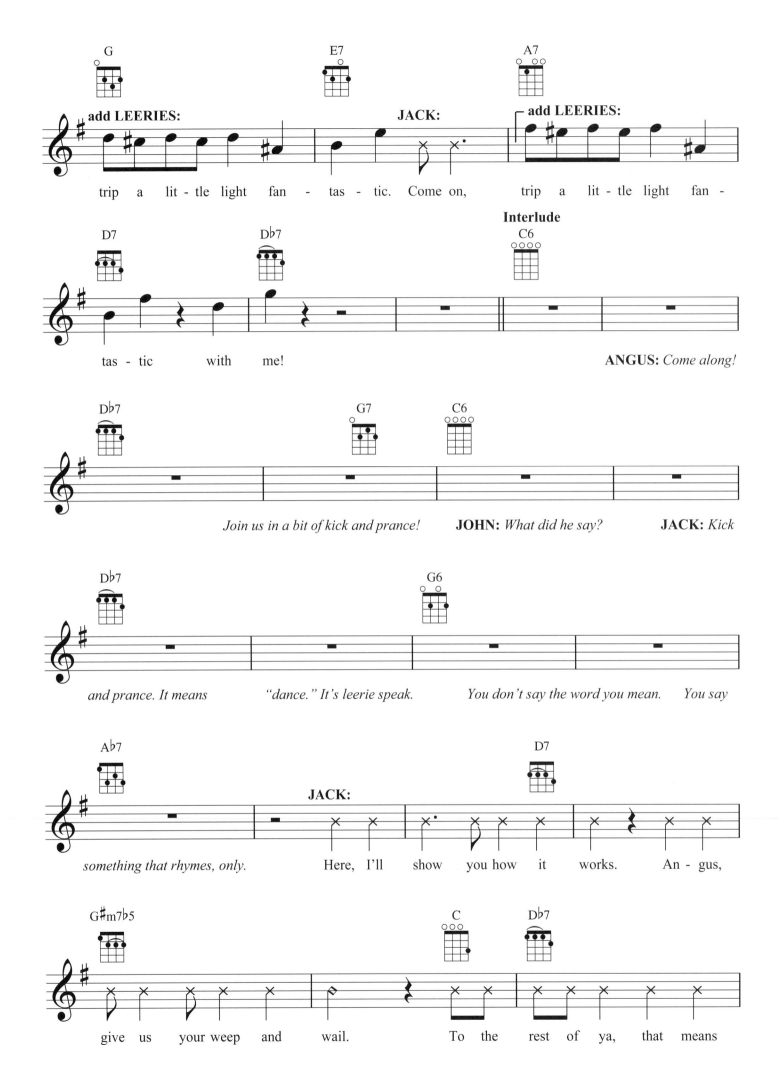

Verse

ANGUS: "tale." 4. I was short of a sheet (He was in the street.) just to

JACK: tum-ble down the sink. (Just to ANGUS: give him-self a drink.) Then I JACK: pinched what's fat-ter (He

ANGUS: grabbed his lad-der.) to JACK: smile and smirk. (To work!)

Interlude

JACK: *You see? There's nothing to it.* ANNABEL: *Can you speak leerie, Mary Poppins?*

MARY: *Can I speak leerie?* JACK: *Of course she can. She's Mary Poppins!*

GEORGIE: *Can we do it with you?* ANNABEL & JOHN: *Please?* MARY: *Oh, very well then.*

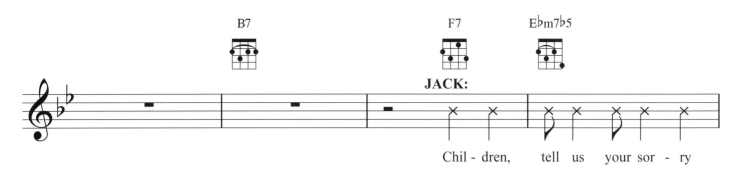

JACK:

Chil - dren, tell us your sor - ry

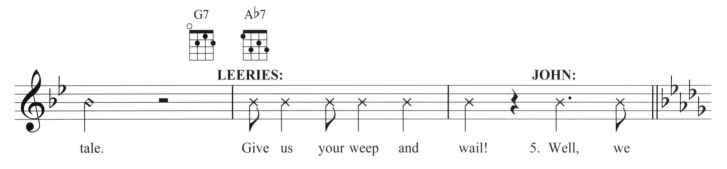

LEERIES: JOHN:

tale. Give us your weep and wail! 5. Well, we

Verse

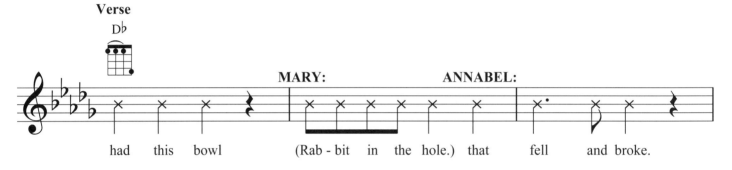

MARY: ANNABEL:

had this bowl (Rab - bit in the hole.) that fell and broke.

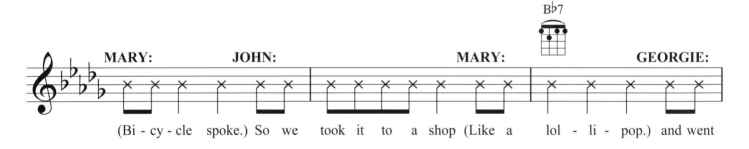

MARY: JOHN: MARY: GEORGIE:

(Bi - cy - cle spoke.) So we took it to a shop (Like a lol - li - pop.) and went

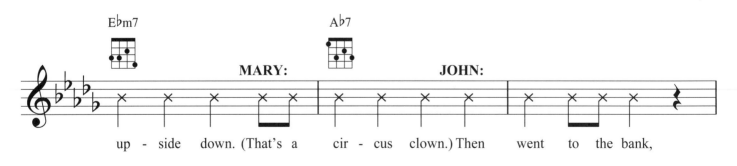

MARY: JOHN:

up - side down. (That's a cir - cus clown.) Then went to the bank,

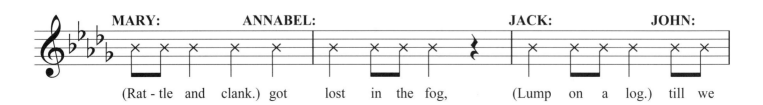

MARY: ANNABEL: JACK: JOHN:

(Rat - tle and clank.) got lost in the fog, (Lump on a log.) till we

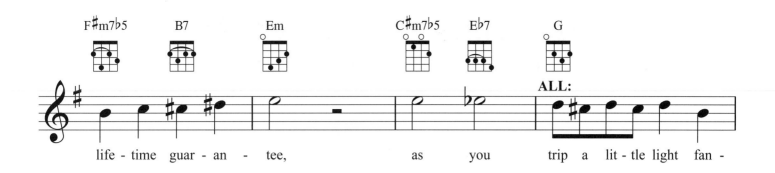

life - time guar - an - tee,   as   you   **ALL:** trip a lit - tle light fan -

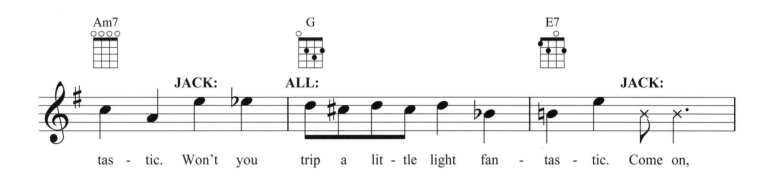

JACK: **ALL:**   **JACK:**

tas - tic. Won't you trip a lit - tle light fan - tas - tic. Come on,

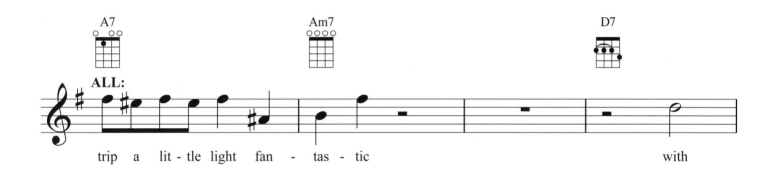

ALL:

trip a lit - tle light fan - tas - tic   with

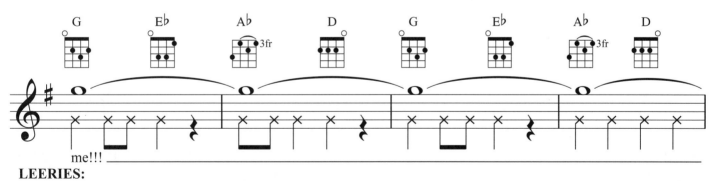

me!!! _____

LEERIES:

(Went to the bank!   Rat - tle and clank!   Met with the boss!   Pitch and toss! Got

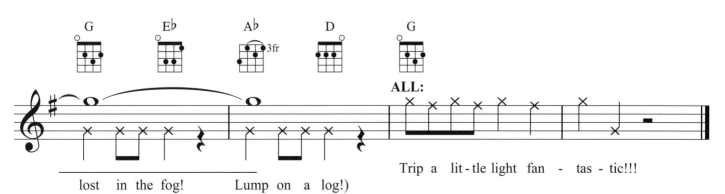

_____   **ALL:**

lost in the fog!   Lump on a log!)   Trip a lit - tle light fan - tas - tic!!!

Nowhere to Go But Up

Music by Marc Shaiman
Lyrics by Scott Wittman and Marc Shaiman

no - where to go but up. Choose the

se - cret we know be - fore life makes us grow. There's

no - where to go but up. If your se -

lec - tion feels right, well then, dear - ie, hold tight. If you

see your re - flec - tion, your heart will take flight. If you

pick the right __ string, then your heart will take __ wing, and there's

Slightly slower

Gm　C7　F

no - where　to　go　but　up.

Interlude
Rubato

F9#11

D♭°7　C°7　D°7　Cm7　F7　**Verse**　B♭

MICHAEL:

2. Now　I　feel　like　that

C#°7　Cm7

boy　with　a　shin - y　new　toy,　and there's　no - where　to

F7sus4　G7　Cm

go　but　up.　Just　one　day　at　the

Cm7　F7　B♭

fair　has　me　waltz - ing　on　air!　And there's　no - where　to

58

go but up.   Now my heart is so

light that I think I just might start feed - ing the

birds, and then go fly a kite! With your head in a

cloud on - ly laugh - ter's al - lowed, and there's no - where to

go but up.

CHILDREN:

3. We're zig - ging and

zag - ging, our feet nev - er drag - ging. We might take a

MICHAEL:

ride to the moon! _____ All this bob - bing and

add CHILDREN:

weav - ing all comes from be - liev - ing the mag - ic in -

JACK:

side the bal - loon. _____ The past is the

past; it lives on as his - t'ry, and that's an im -

por - tant thing. The fu - ture comes

fast,   each   sec - ond   a   mys - t'ry,   for   no - bod - y

knows   what   to - mor - row   may   bring.

Verse

JANE:

4. Up   here   in   the   blue,   it's   a   mar - vel - ous

JACK & JANE:

view!   Side   by   side   is   the   best   way   to   fly.

JACK:

Once   I   just   looked   a - bove,   but   now   I   am   part

of the love - ly Lon - don sky! _____ 5. *(Instrumental)*

Verse

BALLOON LADY:

Well, there's no - where to go but

ELLEN:

up. When the clouds make a muss, well, I

won't make a fuss, but I'll pol - ish the

sleeve. Well, there's no - where to go but up.

As you fly o - ver town it gets hard - er to

frown, and we'll all hit the heights if we nev - er look

MICHAEL:

down. Let the past take a bow: the for - ev - er is

ALL:

now. And there's no - where to go but up.

Up! There's no - where to go but up!